INTRODUCTION

This is the third book in the series about "Kirkcaldy's Famous Folk". Many of the people in this book are famous for their industrial contribution to the town and many have exported their products worldwide. Many of these industrialists have also made generous gifts to Kirkcaldy like Michael Barker Nairn and the Cottage Hospital and Michael Beveridge and the Beveridge Park.

This book also covers the families of the two 'Big Houses' of Kirkcaldy, the Fergusons of Raith and the Oswalds of Dunnikier. Fergusons still live in Raith House but Dunnikier House is now a Hotel.

It is intersting to note that the 'gentry' or heritors have often been educated in England and they have travelled the country and have brought back English wives. The industrialists on the other hand have tended to marry within the local industrial families for example Robert Hutchison married Mary Oliphant, corn joining with shipping. Marriage with the gentry was for the blood line and financial support. The women were but pawns in the game of both groups, bearing numerous children to carry on the line often without success.

Book One covered William and Robert Adam, (father and son), Baillie Robert Philp and his distant relative Dr John Philip, Marjory Fleming and Sir Sandford Fleming, (Last two unrelated)

Book Two covered Adam Smith, Alexander Stewart, Thomas Carlyle, John McDouall Stuart, Anna Buchan, and the Elder family.

Kirkcaldy Harbour c. 1930

Whyte House

Whyt of Bennochy, Greyfriars. 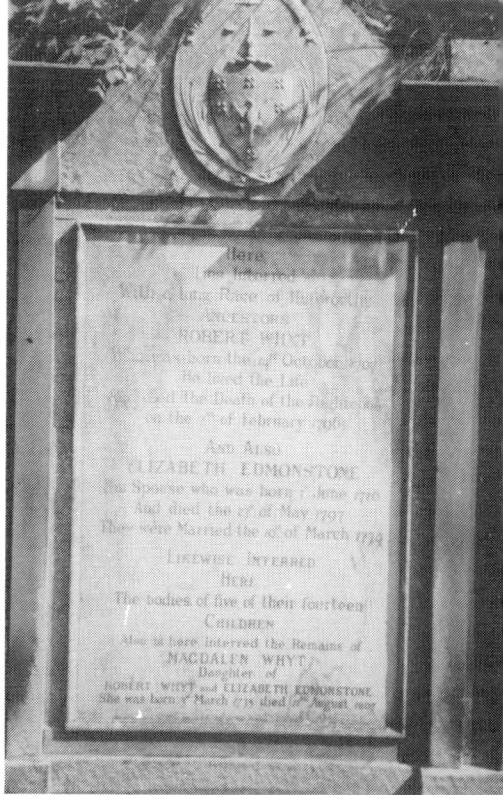   Whyt of Purin, Old Parish Kirk

QUYT or WHYT later WHYTE

Some members of the family claim that their origins were from France around the early 15th Century. There were two Whyt families one of more humble origin than the other. However the two branches of the family were later joined in marriage, and many were leading men in the Civic History of Kirkcaldy. Robert Whyt was several times Provost of Kirkcaldy between 1740 and 1779. Another Provost Robert Whyte was involved with a Court Case in 1876 regarding the sale of parts of the Common Muir (Volunteers' Green) for Municipal Offices.

One of the earliest Whyts mentioned is **John Whyt** a ship master of 1599 and an earlier mention of a **John Whyt** who may have been father of the above also a shipmaster in 1563.

John Whyt of 1599 had two sons, the oldest of whom died and **Robert** the younger one, born in 1599 was much involved in Civic duties being one of the two baillies running the town in 1636, becoming Kirkcaldy's first Provost in 1658

Robert married twice, first **Isobel Law,** daughter of James Law of Dunnikier. She bore him a son and a daughter Isobel. Sadly the son was killed when a barrel of gunpowder exploded and the mother died of shock.

His second wife was **Janet Tennant** of Purin, widow of Henry Miller but with no issue still living, so that later Robert Whyt inherited the lands of Purin. Hence on his gravestone we read "Robert Whyt of Purin, (near Falkland) Provost of Kirkcaldy....".

Robert, born in 1599 died in 1667 aged 68 and his daughter Isobel, the daughter with **Isobel Law Whyt,** married **Thomas Whyt** around 1660 linking the two families. This is the family that also had a large part to play in the history of Kirkcaldy. Isobel and Thomas's grandson was **Provost Robert Whyt** between 1740 and 1779 He married **Elizabeth Edmonstone.** They are buried in the Old Kirk with "five of their fourteen children".

Robert Whyt (1701-1796) built the **Whyte House** which had extensive grounds as parts were later sold:- Whytehouse Mansions 1898, WhytehouseAvenue, Whytescauseway and Whyte Melville Rd. near the station. Sadly Whyte House is about to be demolished.(8/06)

Robert Whyt's son by the second marriage with Janet Tennant **John** 1642-96 died when only 46 but also had two wives. The first was

Jean Melville of Murdocairney; they had three children, sons **Robert, John and Agnes**, who never married. His second wife was **Katherine Arnot**, daughter of David Arnot but there were no children.

It is uncertain at which particular date the lands of Bennochy became a part of the title, 1659 or 1714.

Robert of Bennochy, son of previously mentioned John 1683-1714 died aged 31, yet he had time to father eleven children. He was married to **Jean Murray**. Her grand-daughter married John Adam of Blairadam, Robert Adam's brother.

Robert was succeeded by his second son **George** 1701-28. George studied medicine at Edinburgh University but died in 1828 aged 27 and is buried at Greyfriars Church, in the Covenanters' Prison. His younger brother **Robert,** born after the father had died succeeded him (1714-66). He was Professor of Medicine in Edinburgh. and died aged 52. He married **Lady Lousia Balfour,** daughter of James Balfour of Pilrig and they had fourteen children. He is buried in Greyfriars Graveyard beside his brother George. Robert's granddaughter Helen married Andrew Melville, Minister at Monimail. Through the Melville line the Estate passed to the Whyte Melvilles, thus linking the names of the two families. By 1900 the Estates had passed out of the family.

The Whyte House later became a Temperance Hotel, the first Anthony's Hotel and later was taken over as offices and flats for the Carlton Bakery. This stately List B building, now over 200 years **old is soon to be demolished to make way for a housing development. Sadly is was never visible from the road.**

Old Dunnikier House, now the Path House, a Medical Surgery

Dunnikier House, now Dunnikier Hotel

OSWALD'S of DUNNIKIER

In 1692 John Watson of Burntisland built Dunnikier House in Dunnikier (now known as Pathhead) for his bride Euphan Orrock. Both the date and initials JW and EO are to be seen on the little gables of the south facing upper windows. Today the house is known as the Path House, now a doctors' surgery and the top of the Path became Pathhead when the Oswalds moved away.

However John Watson had overreached himself financially and he sold the house in 1702 to Captain James Oswald.

We first hear of Captain James Oswald (1650-1716), as skipper of a ship and trader at a time when there was a lot of money to be made in such ventures. In 1681 he owned the ship "David" He later became involved in council matters and had no time to sail the seas. He and Henry Oswald (probably brothers) were Provosts of Kirkcaldy and Captain James was one of the MPs at the last sitting of the Scottish Parliament. In 1786 the Oswald Coat of Arms was recognised.

Captain James Oswald married **Isobel Anderson**, daughter of Matthew Anderson and had five surviving children of whom **James Oswald** was the heir born 1685 and died in 1725 aged 40. He married **Anna Durie**, daughter of John Durie and Barbara Hay in 1714 and had six surviving children of whom the oldest was the **Right Honourable James Oswald** (1715-1769) He married in 1746 **Elizabeth Townsend** of Huntingdon Hall, Warwickshire. He was MP for Fife and Kirkcaldy between the years 1741-61. He died in 1769 aged 54.

Their oldest son **James Townsend Oswald** (1748-1814), married **Janet Gray** of Overskibo, Sutherlandshire in 1769, had twelve children and died when he was 64.

James Townsend's second son (first son James died before his father) **John later General Sir John** (1771-1840) married twice, firstly in 1812 to **Charlotte Mary Agnes Murray-Aynsley**, who died in 1827 having had eight children. He married again in 1829 **Amelia Jane Murray**, who had a son and a daughter. He spent many years abroad. His father built around 1790, the new Dunnikier House on the Pathhead Muir. It was from this time on that the area around the new house became known as Dunnikier while the area around the old house became known as it is still today, as Pathhead. General Sir John inherited the mansion house in

7

General Sir James Oswald's Grave, Old Parish Kirk

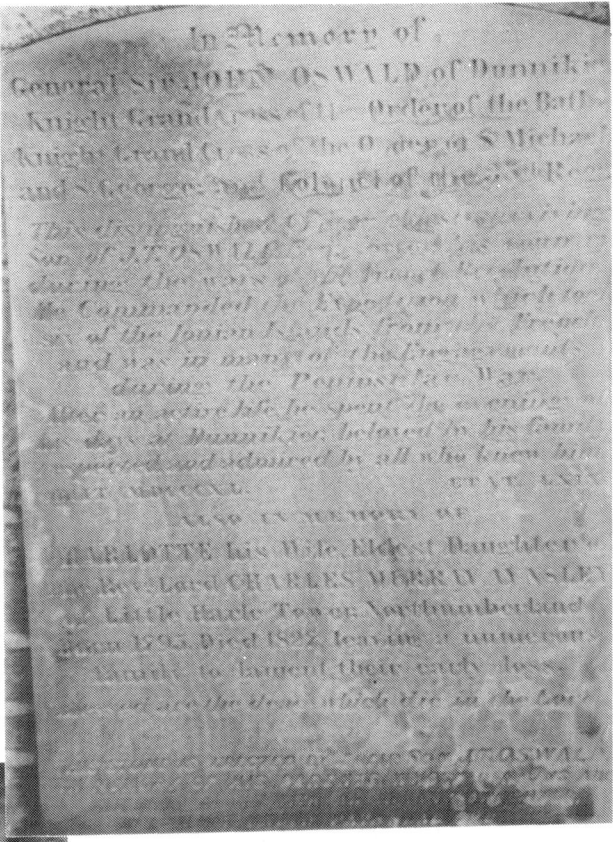

James Townsend Oswald and Colonel St Clair, Bennochy Graveyard

1814 after his father aged 69 had died and it was probably General Sir John's first wife, who certainly had French connections through her mother, who refused to live in the house. (It is said that 'a French Oswald Wife' refused to live in the house).

The General served in the Napoleonic wars, was secretary and clerk on the Leeward Islands, (West Indies) and retired to Dunnikier House, which his father James built.

The General's second son James, born in 1820 succeeded, the first son having died as an infant. James married the English **Ellen Octavia Miles** (1821-1907) of Leigh Court and Kingsweston in 1848 and they had five daughters and two sons.. He died in 1893 aged 73

James was succeeded firstly by his son John born 1856, but John never married and died in 1927 aged 71. The line then passed to James' second son (brother of John) Colonel St Clair (1858-1938) He had married **Elizabeth Winifred Osborne** from St Ives in Huntingtonshire in 1915 and they had only one daughter **Daphne** born in 1920. Colonel St Clair died in 1938 aged 80. Elizabeth Winifred Osborne was not interested in Dunnikier House, died in 1973.

General Sir John Townsend Oswald and his wife were buried in the Crypt of Pathhead Parish Church, built as a Chapel-of-Ease in 1823 to save the people walking all the way to Dysart for worship. This was then the Parish Church for Dunnikier/Pathhead.

There is a gravestone in the Old Parish Graveyard to the memory of **Lieut. Col. Robert Oswald** youngest son of James Townsend, and his wife Janet Gray,1784-1848. He was wounded at the taking of the Ionian Islands (Greece) and died aged 64 years.

The Oswald family lived for nearly a hundred years in the first Dunnikier House and then they decided to build a town house so they could be involved in Council affairs. In 1763, they sold the Path House and built a house in the High Street on the south corner of Dishington Wynd, which was later renamed Oswald's Wynd. This house was demolished when the Co-op was built in 1903. Later part of the rear garden was sold to Mr Russell to build his house 'The Terrace' in 1870. This house was demolished in 1995 for the building of Church Court.

In 1790 the Oswalds built a new mansion up on what was called Pathhead Muir. These lands they had acquired from the Lundins of Balgonie and the Laws of Dunnikier. The family continued to live for 150 years at 'Dunnikier House', which has a beautiful Adam fireplace.

The land extended right to the boundary of Kirkcaldy and included the lands of Balsusney. Dunnikier Primary School was built on land from the estate, McIntosh acquired his ground from the family and the High Level (Smithy's Bar) was until the 1950's the highest level from the sea that the Oswalds would grant a license.

Dunnikier House was sold to Kirkcaldy Town Council in 1945 and later was leased and converted into a hotel. The house no longer belongs to the Council.

Much of the land from the Estate has been sold for industry and houses. Many streets in Kirkcaldy have been named after members of the family:-Townsend Place and Crescent after Elizabeth Townsend (1698-1779); John Street after General Sir John Oswald; Winifred Street, wife of Colonel St Clair; Octavia Street named after the wife of James Oswald; Lina Street said to be named after James Townsend's youngest daughter; Katherine Street as in 1810 the Earl of Elgin married Katherine one of the daughters of the family; Montgomery named after one member of the family. Whyteman's Brae was so named as the butler to the family, Edward Whyteman had a little cottage here. Dunnikier Road and Oswald Road show the extent of the Estate.

There were seven generations of Oswalds of Dunnikier inheriting in a direct line from father to son, except for one instance where it passed from brother to brother. This was over a period of two hundred and fifty years.

The Council sold ground for the building of the houses at Dunnikier Estate, created a Park, a golf course, and a caravan park.

Much coal was found beneath the lands of Dunnkier and this was mined and made a very profitable investment in the mid-nineteenth Century. There was the Lina Pit and Dunnikier Colliery and the evidence of these coal workings is till apparent today in spoil heaps up the side of Johnny Marshall's Loan. Johnny Marshall, incidently was a farrier who carted coal down to the Harbour. There are also sealed up shafts on the fields behind Duddingston Drive.

The Oswalds also owned several saltpans around the Harbour area, which ceased in the 18th and early 19th Centuries, leaving the 'bucket pats', water resevoirs, now long since gone.

The fact that two houses on Dunnikier Estate recently had to be demolished due to mining subsidence as well as a block at the corner of Alexandra Street and West Albert Road is partly due to the fact that the main Dunnikier workings were extensive and remain mostly uncharted.

Raith House

Evanton Graveyard

FERGUSON'S of RAITH

Raith Estate has been owned by the Fergusons of Raith since the death of the first Earl of Melville in the early 18th Century.

The first **William Ferguson** of Raith married around 1730 **Jane Crauford** daughter of Ronald Crauford of Restalrig., (near Edinburgh). Her sister was the Countess of Dalkeith.

Their son, **Robert Crauford Ferguson** was MP for Kirkcaldy from 1767-1840 and died in London aged 73.

Robert Crauford Ferguson's oldest son was **General Sir John Ferguson** of Nottingham who died without having an heir. His brother **Sir Ronald Ferguson** was the next heir of Raith who was born in Raith House in 1773 and died in 1840 aged 68. He married **Jane the daughter of Sir Hector Munro of Novar, Ross-shire** who died in 1830. The name Munro Ferguson has continued to this day, although there have had to be some name adoptions for purposes of inheritance.

Sir Ronald's son, **Ronald Munro-Ferguson** was born in Raith House in 1860. He had a sister Miss Munro-Ferguson who was living in Raith House in 1894. He was a Liberal MP for Ross and Cromarty in 1884 and private Secretary to Lord Rosebery. Later he was MP for Leith. He married in 1889 **Lady Helen Hermione,** eldest daughter of **Lord Dufferin and Ava** and became Governor General of Australia. He had received his peerage in 1920 and chose the title **Viscount Novar.** He died at Raith House in 1934 aged 74. There is a plaque just inside Abbotshall Church to "Ronald Viscount Novar Laird of Raith, Chief Heritor and elder in this parish...."

After a funeral service in Abbotshall Church the coffin was taken by train for cremation in Edinburgh. The Press of that time tell us that the flowers were placed in the private burial ground on the Raith Estate, before the coffin was taken to Edinburgh..

Viscount Novar was survived by his widow, a JP who was much involved in charitable works. There were no children so the Estate passed to his brother **General Sir Robert Munro Ferguson.**

General Sir Robert married **Emma the daughter of Henry Manderville** of Merton, Surrey in 1889. but again there were no children..

The title was not hereditary but the Estate now passed to the Viscount's sister's son **Mr Arthur Brocklehurst Luttrell** who in

Torbain Tower

Lambswell "church gable" and ruined cottage.

Follies Around Raith House.. Trees obscure view from Raith House

Balwearie cottage with "church gable", by the golf course.

order to inherit had to assume the name **Arthur Munro-Ferguson.** This was recognised by the Lord Lyon in 1951. He was the son of Ralph Paganel Luttrell and Alice Brocklehurst. In 1952 he married **Jane Euphemia Beatrice** daughter of Lewis Reynold of Natal. There were two sons and two daughters of the marriage which was dissolved in 1980 after which he married **Mary Griselda** daughter of William Robertson,. She was the former wife of John Chubb.

Today the Novar estates are looked after by Arthur Munro-Ferguson's sons of Raith and Novar. The younger son Richard lives in Raith House, Kirkcaldy while the older brother looks after the Novar Estates.

Some members of the Munro-Fergusons family are buried in Evanton Churchyard in Sutherland.

Much of the Raith Estate has been sold off. In 1890 a part was sold for the Beveridge Park and the Mill Dam still technically belongs to the Estate. Hence when new regulations about the maintenance of dams were introduced by the E.C. and neither Fife Regional Council nor Kirkcaldy District would undertake any responsibilty for care and maintenance, the dam was burst and the Mill Dam became a stream running through an area of very dangerous mud.

Houses at Raith Estate, and Long Braes have been built on land from the Raith Estate. Ground was sold in some of the older parts of the town for housing and the streets were named after members of the family. Both Ava Street and Lady Helen Street are named after Lady Helen wife of Sir Ronald Crawford Munro Ferguson. Falloden Crescent was named after Viscount Gray of Falloden, a friend of Sir Ronald Munro Ferguson,. Cloanden Crescent was named afer Richard Haldane who came from the village of Cloanden in Perthshire, and who was also a friend of Sir Ronald Munro Ferguson.

Ferrard Road was named after a descendant of the Melvilles of Raith who married one of the Whytes of Bennochy, while Massereen Road was named after Lord Massereen (Sir John Clotsworthy) second Viscount Ferrard whose wife Florence Whyte Melville owned land in Kirkcaldy.

Raith House, 500 feet (150 metres) above sea level, was built in 1684 by Alexander, Lord Raith, eldest son of George the First Earl of Melville, for his bride Barbara Dundas The wings were added later. The Tower which once held a unique geological collection, is older than the house and was probably built for defence. Perhaps there was once a Castle on what is now called 'Castle Hill'. Raith Lake was created in 1812, but the Mill Dam being used for water power for the mills, is much older.

Bennochy House

Townsend Cottage

MALCOLM'S OF KIRKCALDY

John Malcolm, shipowner in Kirkcaldy was born in 1745 and died in 1825 at the age of 80 and is buried in the Old Parish Church with his wife Elizabeth Smith, who had died in 1812 at the age of 71. Six of their children **Alexander, Francis** and **George** are mentioned on the gravestone including the three who predeceased them, James, Elizabeth and Grace. John Malcolm's address is given as 5 East Brae or 465 High Street today, where there is a house called Malcolm's House.

Francis was a timber merchant at Port Brae living in the High Street in 1820 and at Harbourhead in 1825. He died in 1834.

Alexander John's son was born in 1777, also a ship builder and shipowner died in 1844 at the age of 76. His wife was Janet Alison who died in 1855 aged 83, They had six children a son **James** who died in Adelaide in 1865 aged 56, who had been employed by the Elders also from Kirkcaldy. Also Andrew, John, Alex, Betsy and Jessie.

George Senior, late shipbuilder and shipowner, 1771-1836 also son of John Malcolm and Elizabeth Smith, married **Isabella Greig,** 1777-1813, who died in 1813 aged 36. He later married again, **Mary Morrison.** He died aged 65. George and Isabella had three sons **David, George Junior and Alexander Greig,**

George Junior son of the above George Malcolm, was born in 1800 He was twice Provost of Kirkcaldy between 1828 and 1834. However George Junior pioneered a new line of business for the family as ships and ship building of sailing vessels were being overtaken by steamships. In 1836 he bought the Mill at Coal Wynd, built by Ebenezer Birrell, from Robert Mitchell and in 1856 put in coal-fired machinery. He sold out to the Swan brothers in 1870 and retired to Bennochy House

Alexander Greig Malcolm was born in December 1813 three weeks before his mother died He is noted for being a member of the Free Church of Scotland that left the Old Parish Church in 1843 and set up a new Church in Tolbooth Street. When this grew too small for the expanding congregation they moved in 1881 to the large St Brycedale Church. He was an important member of the Church Committee selecting a new minister in 1866. He died in 1895 aged 82. He was married to **Janet Kinninmonth** (1836-1897) daughter of the Lothrie Lemonade Works. They had two daughters and a son.

George Malcolm of Bennochy House

Malcolm Gravestones **Old Kirk graveyard**

Janet Kinninmonth died 1897 and the youngest daughter Janet Alexandra was born in 1875. Their son **George** was born in 1860 and died in 1928 aged 68.

George married **Anna Pye Dunbar** of Townsend Cottage, Kirkcaldy. Their two children were born in Townsend Cottage, **George** born in 1907, became a poultry farmer in the south of England and **Mary,** who married Abram Douglas, had two sons. It is thought that George and Anna Malcolm later moved to Woodbine Cottage, where Mrs Malcolm lived after her husband died. This cottage was associated with and was beside the Lemonade Works. The Kinnimonths, George's grandmother, had been associated with the Lothrie Lemonade business, which moved after the Lothrie Water Works were opened, to a site adjacent to Woodbine Cottage.

George, son of George and Anna married **Mary Lovelace** and also had two sons, one who went to the Argentine while the other went to New Zealand where he died leaving two sons, one Kit who has twice come to Kirkcaldy to search out his roots. He is now (1999) about 29.

There are four Malcolm graves in the Old Parish Kirkyard, John, Alexander, Alexander Greig, George Senior.

Malcolm's Wynd is near where the ship building used to be and connects the High Street with St Mary's Road. There is a house on the High street named **Malcolm's House,** with a dated lintel.

Fosterton Farm 1997.

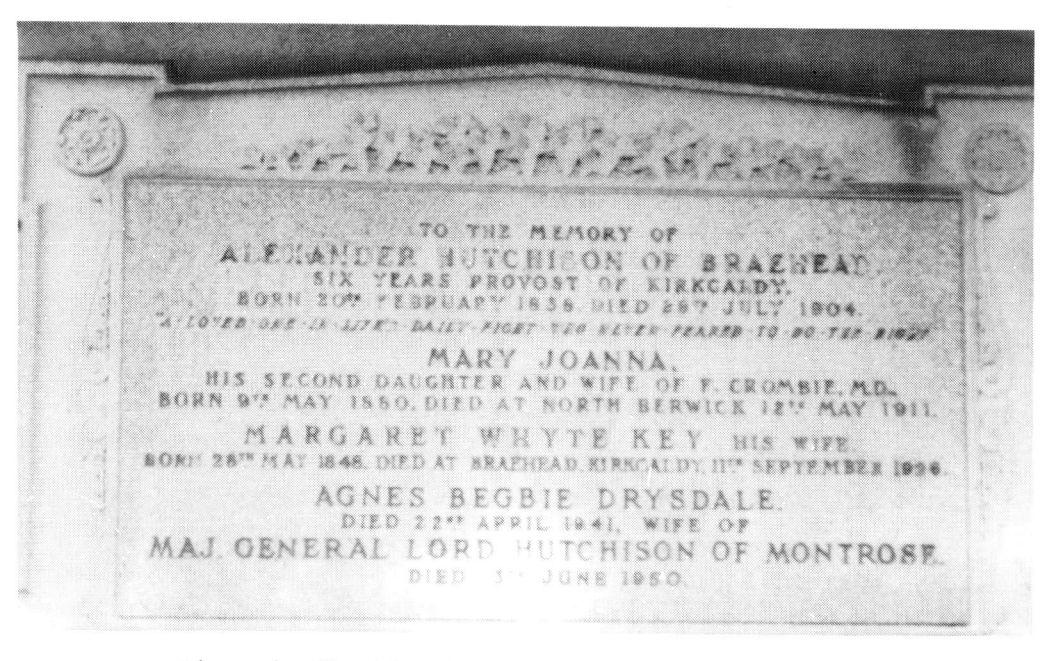

Alexander Hutchison's Gravestone, Bennochy Cemetery

HUTCHISONS of KIRKCALDY

In 1746 **John Hutchison** leased Fosterton Farm, Thornton from Raith Estate and the lease continued with the Hutchison family until 1916.

In 1779 he acquired a share in a building in the High Street near the Old Tolbooth or Town House. The occupation of the family was described as Fleshers and Corn Millers, they combined farming with retail, with a business set up in the High Street, John Hutchison and Co. John Hutchison died in 1804 and the business was carried on by his son **Alexander.**

Alexander married **Johan Binnie** of Crammond. They had four daughters and five sons Her father was a glazier but it appears that the family were also living in the High Street. Alexander lived at Fosterton Farm. He died in 1834

Other sons of John Hutchison, **John and Thomas** continued in the business after their father had died but unfortunately went bankrupt in 1839, although John died when he was relativly young.

Robert the second son of Alexander had long before set up on his own as a corn merchant with a shop in the High Street established 1826 and took in his uncle Thomas in 1844 from the bankrupt business. Later with his brother-in-law he acquired premises at the East Bridge, which was then the property of a Distiller. It was converted by Robert and his brother-in-law into a flour mill.

In 1837 when he was 32, Robert married his long time sweetheart **Mary Oliphant** then 30, the daughter of the Oliphants of shipowner fame who lived at the East Toll next to the house of James Ferguson of Raith ie at Sailors Walk which at that time consisted of four flats, three of which belonged to the Oliphant Family. The house was often known as Oliphant House. The Oliphants were known to have been Jacobites.

Robert and Mary's first son **Alexander** was born in 1838. There were three sons and five daughters. Shortly after the last one was born in 1851 Mary was unwell and it transpired that she had tuberculosis. She was sent to the south of England with her friend and companion Jessie Thomson for rest and recovery. On her way home nearly two years later, in 1853, she sadly died. In 1857 Robert married **Jessie** Thomson.

Robert had bought Cowan's Brewery, the Knowe, Braehead Cottages, Spears Distillery from Hemsworth who did not seem to know what to do with his new business and the Holmes which

Hutchison's Office, The Path.

Hutchison's Works. Maltings now closed. Flour Mill by Harbour.
New Sewage works have been built on the site.

included Jock's Road of which there was later a Court case regarding the flooding of water from Hutchisons to the Road. The case against John Heggie the Dyer, went to court and Robert Hutchison won the case. It is surprising that Robert had not bought Heggie out earlier. Before leaving Fosterton Farm Robert had invented a new turnip the Fosterton Hybrid Turnip.

In 1847 Robert bought Braehead House which had been built in 1795. Robert was a workaholic and not only was he involved with milling and malting but he was involved with speculative buying which included much grain from the Black Sea at the time of the Crimean War 1856-57, when some cargoes of wheat were lost. They lost heavily and the banks were not keen to advance money. There was also a cattle disease in 1866 and a bad harvest.

Robert's second son Bob was killed in a fox hunting accident. **Alexander**, first son and **Henry William**, his third son were left to run the business. Things were looking very gloomy as the firm was well in the red and the banks were not keen to advance any money.

However by 1870 Hutchison's Maltings and Mill were considered to be the largest in Scotland

An **Alleyn Nicolson** "of the University of Toronto", married one of Robert's daughters **Isabella.Hutchison**. Alleyn Nicolson's son was later involved with Stocks linen. and became Provost of Kirkcaldy in the 1970's.

In 1872 Alexander married **Margaret Whyt Key** daughter of John Key of the Whitebank Engineering Works which shortly after had grave financial problems. He was 34 and she 24. They had a son in 1873, **John Key** who carried on in the family business. Margaret Whyt Key died at Braehead House in 1926 aged 82. Around 1937 Robert Huchison sold Braehead House to the Nairns. The house was demolished and the new office block for Nairns was built, which served as Head Office for over fifty years. The building has now been converted to luxury flats. The Society now has a photograph of Braehead House dated about 1900.

In 1884 the mill and maltings were refitted with new machinery and no more investment was needed until 1932. Alexander ran the flour mill and Henry the Maltings. Henry bought Eastbank House, Loughborough Road from the Earl of Rosslyn in 1902.

Alexander's son **Robert** became **Lord Hutchison of Montrose** after a brilliant army career ending up as Major-General. He married **Agnes Begbie Drysdale** who died in 1941.

John Key Hutchison joined the Board of Directors in 1896

Braehead House

Prinlaws Mill, Leslie. (Now demolished)

Alexander died suddenly of a heart attack in 1904. He had been Provost of Kirkcaldy from 1896-1904, a time when tramways were introduced to Kirkcaldy and the population was expanding rapidly. Henry now became Chairman until died in 1922. In 1926 the firm celebrated its Centenary

Lieut. Colonel R.G.O. Hutchison, of Cunnoquhie, Alexander's nephew, now became the new Chairman, but in 1934 he died aged only 47 and is buried in Monimail Cemetery. He married **Ruth Gordon** and had commanded the 7th Meerut Division Machine Gun Battalion, serving in Poland 1916-18. Major-General Lord Ronald Hutchison of Montrose became the new Chairman and died in 1950. In 1937 there was an extensive fire at the Maltings.

1939 The Directors **Mr A.O Hutchison** and **Mr Hutchison Turion** went to join the Fife and Forfar Yeomanry and went off to the war In 1943 **Robert** eldest son of John Key Hutchison was killed. during World War II.

In 1951 **Alex. Hutchison** oldest son of Mr A.O. Hutchison became the next Chairman..

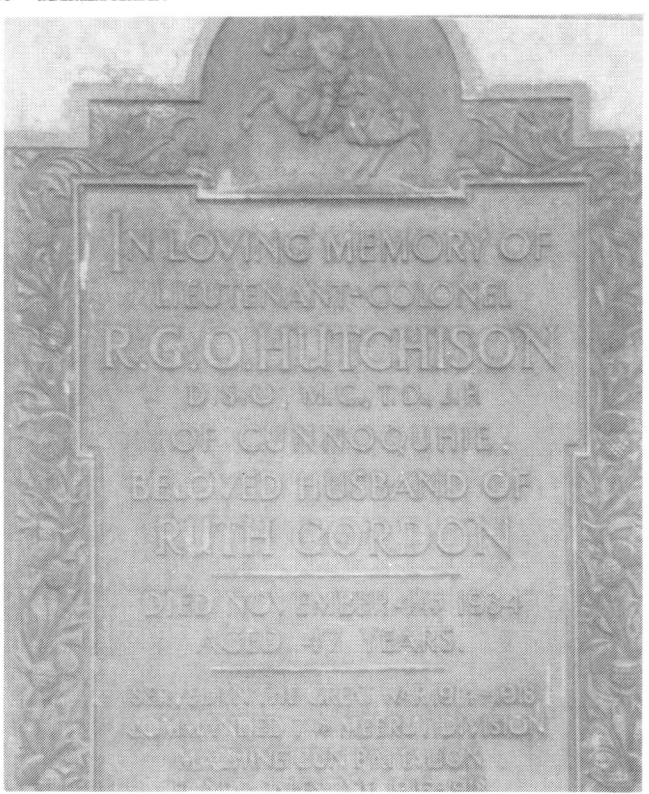

Grave of Lieut. Col. R.G.O. Hutchison, Monomail Graveyard

Strathore House

Grave of Walter Fergus and Charlotte Bruce Whyt

FERGUS FAMILY

John Fergus came as a weaver from Newburgh to the west Links. His shop in which he lodged had a cow behind the bed which was not unusual in those days. He had two sons James and Walter. Walter Fergus (1760-1830), had a linen factory where Stocks is today, on the junction of Fergus Wynd with Links Street.

Walter Fergus married **Charlotte Bruce Whyt** and had a son **John.** Walter was Provost of Kirkcaldy several times between 1793 and 1826. and he lived in the Whyte House in Kirkcaldy, Sadly this house although listed is soon to be demolished. In 1795 Walter was known to have held a ball here and it was here that Marjory Fleming's parents, Isobel Bremner and James Fleming first met. Walter later bought and lived at Strathore House, which still stands in Thornton. On his gravestone in the Old Kirk he is described as Walter Fergus of Strathore. A marble bust was made of Walter Fergus and given to the town It is now in Kirkcaldy Museum's store.

Walter Fergus's son John owned a mill at Redford while, Walter his father had interests in Linktown and Kinghorn, when in 1828 John branched out into Prinlaws having bought the Milldeans and the Old Mill from John Melville who had overstretched himself financially. By 1836 he employed 320 and by 1858 1500. The business was known as John Fergus and Co. Ltd. In 1836 he built the West Mill and in 1853 the North Mill. The factory was considered a model works as far as success and the welfare of the workers was concerned, with a school and workers' houses. While John Fergus was interested in the welfare of his workers he was not concerned enough to reduce the working week from 56 hours for six days. The factory continued until 1957 when the mill went into liquidation and closed. Now, after many years lying empty, all the buildings have been demolished and houses have been built.

The Prinlaws School for workers children and half-timers still remains in Leslie as a church hall. In 1854 we are told that there were 60 pupils, including half-timers.

John Fergus was a bachelor and every day rode out of Kirkcaldy to his Prinlaw Works. He had earlier been an MP for Kirkcaldy, but resigned in 1859 when there was a slump in the linen trade, so that he could concentrate on his business

It is interesting to note that John Fergus was well enough respected to have the John Fergus School of today (for problem pupils) named after him. The Fergus Places, East, West, South and North were named after the Fergus family as is Fergus Wynd on the Links.

Ninian Lockhart and Sons' mill in Links Street, Burleigh Street

Bennochy Works of Ninian Lockhart 1860

NINIAN LOCKHART.
1775-1848

Ninian Lockhart left the farming community he was brought up in, in Newburgh in 1797 when he was 22 years old and came to Kirkcaldy and settled in Linktown where he set up a small weaving business. As he was not in the Royal Burgh of Kirkcaldy he could not sell his product in Kirkcaldy and so he would walk to markets in Dundee and Perth to sell his cloth rising at 3 or 4 am, returning late the same day. He was hard-working and his business prospered and soon on the site of his hand-weaving shop he set up at a small factory which grew and grew.

Around 1795 he married **Catherine Peddie**, daughter of Mr Peddie, a Baptist pastor from Edinburgh. Catherine died in 1814 aged 40. They had two sons **David** 1795-1860 and **Ninian Lockhart** born in 1801 and a daughter **Elizabeth** born in 1806, who became the wife of James Goodall. Elizabeth died in 1855 aged 49. Ninian Lockhart Senior married again to **Alison Pratt** who died in Philadelphia aged 91 in 1871 (born 1780). Ninian and Alison had two sons **John** 1818-1909 and **Robert** 1822-1902 who became involved in the business and a daughter **Annie Louse**. Ninian Senior was a staunch Baptist and became a lay preacher, deacon and later elder in the early Baptist Church in Rose Street. He was a liberal thinker, also actively supported the anti-slavery movement. Ninian Senior died in 1848 aged 73.

Ninian Lockhart Junior set up his own business around 1850. He was so successful that he was able to build his own four storey spinning factory in 1864 opposite Abbotshall Church, the Bennochy Works, which closed in 1984 and was demolished in 1986. He was a member also of the Scotch Baptist Church in Rose Street and was a lay preacher. He married **Ann Douglas** and had a large family four of whom died before they were 6 years old. His sons **George** and **James** entered his business., but his son **William** left Kirkcaldy when he was a young married man and went to Liverpool when his son **William Peddie** was 12 years old. William Peddie became a well known Baptist preacher and merchant commission agent in Liverpool. Ninian Lockhart Junior died in the Whyte House in 1880, when he was 80 years old.

John Lockhart had two sons. The oldest was **Robert Cook Lockhart** who later moved to Edinburgh and later became **Sir Robert Lockhart** (1861-1948) who was a Provost of Kirkcaldy,

1914-18. He had three sons one of whom, **Jack Sutherland** 1898-1916 died in action in the first World War and the second **Robert Brady** died in 1932 several years later as a result of wounds then received. His third son **William** had emigrated to Canada but returned between the Wars to help to run the business. Robert who died in 1889 aged 71 married **Ann Davies**

Of the third generation the other son **Robert Brady** had one son **George Barclay** but he too, sadly died during the First World War 1893-1917.

William's son, of the fourth generation **Thomas Kyd Lockhart** was the one who sadly had to see the works closed in 1980 and demolished shortly after. The site was sold to what was Comet now Dunelm although the Lockhart office block still survives. Thomas Lockhart's three sons, now the fifth generation, are in various occupations, **Michael Ninian, Robert William and Alan Thomas Clark** but the last named remains in the linen business as Managing Director of Peter Greig, Kirkcaldy, now the only linen manufacturer left in Fife.(2006)

Lockhart Graves, Abbotshall

Grave of James Aytoun and his children, Abbotshall Kirkyard

44 Nicol Street and 46, Newton House

The mills were demolished in 1998 and retirement flats have been built on the site.

Newton Mills, Nicol Street 1992

JAMES EDMONSTOUNE AYTOUN
1775-1864

James Aytoun was born in Edinburgh. At 17 in 1792 James went to Manchester to learn about the thriving cotton business there. While in England he discovered in Darlington a new patent for spinning flax and returned in 1797 with a license, setting up a spinning mill in Kinghorn. He used the water power from the loch, but the loch was quickly drained so he set up one of the first coal steam-generated mills, but there seemed no profit in the venture and in 1801 he abandoned the works; he was ahead of his time. Later the Swan Brothers took over these works.

James then worked in a bank for a while and then went to the Haugh Spinning Mill Balcurvie, where he was a manager for seven years, then moving on to Neilson's and Co., Spinning Works, Kirkland where he met his wife as the mill was owned by the Peter family. He married **Mary Peter,** born in Dundee and in 1821, bought the small spinning mill in Newton (Nicol Street) from William Greig. Shortly after it went on fire. However he built three new mills there, the first in 1822 the Thistle Mill, the second in 1825 the Rose Mill and the third in 1842 the Shamrock Mill. This time he was able to use steam power with great success. Aytoun's Mills closed around 1870, but James Aytoun had been very successful and has been called the Father of Spinning (in Fife). In 1861 he lived at 44 Nicol Street. At that time he had a son James living at home, aged 43, described as a "fund-holder", a daughter Mary aged 45 and a son Roger described as a "master flax-spinner". There had been nine children in total, born between 1812-1830, many of whom died young. James Aytoun was a member of Abbotshall Parish Church, gifting the Church beautiful stained glass windows.

There was an oil seed cake works on the site, later Lile's brush factory from around 1860, which moved to Charlotte Street in 1884, Rose Street in 1895, finally closing altogether in 1940. Hogg's shoe factory and repair department was on the site for a number of years. However the chief user of the works was George Halley's dyeworks which moved in in 1920 and continued on the site until the business closed in 1984. There have been three generations of George Halleys, dyers in Linktown. The founder of the dyeworks came to Kirkcaldy from Leith in 1853 and worked for Heggie in the Links. When Heggie died his son ran the works for a short while until George Halley bought over the business in 1874. The remaining buildings of the Newton Mills were demolished in 1998.

Offices at the Path, Grecian Style

Monimail Cemetery. Barker Nairn and Spencer Nairn Graves

MICHAEL NAIRN

1804-1858

Michael Nairn was born in Kirkcaldy in 1804 the third son of **James Nairn**. His father came from a family of master weavers and indeed Michael's great grandfather **Andrew Nairn** had been Deacon of the Guild of Weavers and his grandfather **Robert** had also been involved in the weaving trade.

For Michael's father times were hard then and much of the linen and weaving trade had been ruined by the loss of markets following the America's Declaration of Independence in 1776, so that James Nairn was at one time a grocer and at another a shoemaker, and was not involved in the linen trade but he was obviously still well-connected as he married **Isobel Barker** sister of **Michael Barker** shipowner and linen manufacturer of Kirkcaldy, whose grave is in the Old Parish Church with mention of his many brothers and sisters of which Isobel Barker was one of at least twelve. Isobel and James must have lived somewhere within the Royal Burgh of Kirkcaldy and had ten children of which Michael was the third son. James Nairn became a burgess of the Royal Burgh of Kirkcaldy in 1786 and a Burgess of Kinghorn in 1790.

Catherine Ingram...Mrs Nairn

Michael Nairn's First Factory, Hill Street 1828. Canvas Factory

Michael Nairn was destined for the weaving trade which after the end of the Seven Years War 1756-63, between Austria and Germany and following Napoleonic Wars from the end of the eighteenth Century until 1815 saw the trade again beginning to pick up.

As a boy Michael Nairn must have watched the ships coming into the Harbour loaded with flax from the Baltic Countries and also some hemp. Flax growing in Scotland had died out as Baltic imports were cheap and easy to get.

Michael was first apprenticed to a firm in Dundee alongside a young man James Cox who later became one of the pioneer jute barons of Dundee. Michael later returned and set up a small weaving factory in the Linktown of Abbtshall, where at the age of 21 in 1825 he was listed as one of ten linen manufacturers in the area, Robert Philp and James Aytoun being two of the ten..

In 1828 Michael Nairn moved back into the Royal Burgh of Kirkcaldy, bought a house at the Port Brae on Old Main Street near the Harbour and built a four storey canvas factory at the top of his garden with an entrance from Hill Street.

The factory building became the Travel Club after World War II and closed in the mid 1970's as there were financial difficulties. After a fire the building was demolished around 1990 and new houses built on the site but the 1828 stone has been retained on a plinth outside the gatehouse of the Forbo-Nairn Works.

The first canvas factory appeared in Kirkcaldy in 1811. Michael Nairn bought yarn from men like James Aytoun, regarded as the 'Father of Spinning' in Fife, also from Swan, Millie, Fergus and Landale. While Michael Nairn was successful and made a profit selling canvas world-wide, he had the wisdom to see the writing on the wall, that sailing ships were being rapidly replaced by steamships and the market for sail cloth canvas would soon dry up. Michael's interest was in the new floorcloths.

A few years after setting up in the Port Brae Michael Nairn married **Catherine Ingram** in 1836. She was the daughter of Alexander Ingram of St Marys' Bleachfields. As a young girl Catherine had collected pennies from the local people bleaching their linen on Ingam bleachfields. The young Nairns moved from old Main Street to 18 High Street. Uncle Michael Barker was a neighbour. It was a good match, Catherine understanding the business and aiding her husband with frugal housekeeping. There was a total of eight children of whom five survived, three sons and two daughters.

Nairn's Folly opened 1847, first Scottish Floorcloth Factory

St Mary's after Michael Barker Nairn's additions ie third floor.

Robert was born in 1837, followed by **Michael Barker** in 1839, **Euphemia** in 1842, **Isabella Barker** in 1850 and the youngest **John** born in 1854. There were three sons who died young, James second son died 1852 aged seven and one day later Peter Barker, third son aged 4, also their youngest son Andrew.

The floorcloth market was what Michael Nairn wanted into. He had visited factories in England where there were at least twelve while at that time there were none in Scotland and the opportunity was there for Michael Nairn which he seized. He was 40 when he started to think of building his new factory which opened in 1847. He had a wife and three young children.

Michael Nairn planned his floorcloth factory for Pathhead (Dunnikier) which was then outside the boundary of Kirkcaldy until 1876. At this time Sinclairtown Station had just opened in 1847.

Michael Nairn did not make a large profit and so he had to rely heavily on bank loans for his large new factory "Nairns Folly", built on the sands at Pathhead. Added to this it was going to take several months of slow drying before the new floorcloth could be sold. It dried with the sun's heat from the south facing windows. All the work at this time being done by hand, there being as yet no machinery. In point of fact it was early 1849 before the first sales took place. There were no partners or private backers, and wages had to be paid throughout this time. The bank must have had complete confidence in his project for they loaned all the money required. Later a system of hot air ventilation reduced the many months of the drying process.

English floorcloth had been patented by Nathan Smith in 1763 and in 1863 linoleum by Fredrick Walton who after over ten years forgot to register again the patent in 1876. Linoleum then became a household word and all the floorcloth manufacturers used the magic word.

Scottish Floorcloth was exhibited at the Great Exhibition in Crystal Palace of 1851 but won no awards. However in 1862 in the Great Exhibition in the South Kensington Museum Nairns Floorcloth came into its own but by this time Michael Nairn was dead. Again at the Paris Exhibition of 1867 Nairn's Linoleum won top awards.

Michael Nairn died on January 18 1858 he was 54 and Catherine Ingram, his widow was but 43 years old. This was a crucial time and the business robbed of its helmsman could easily have failed.

At this time Robert Nairn was 22 and not altogether strong and robust, Michael Barker was 19 and John but 4. However Mrs Nairn became a partner and leased the firm back to three partners on a

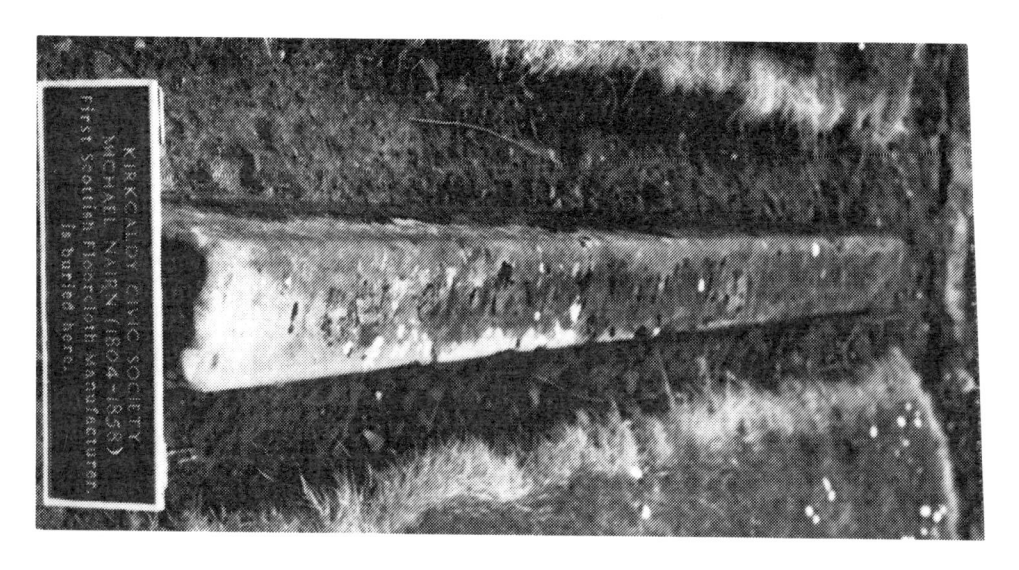

Michael Nairn's Grave, Old Parish Church, includes his parents, two unmarried aunts and three of Michael Nairn's infant sons.

Catherine Ingram's (Nairn) Grave and that of Robert and the daughters, Isabella and Euphemia.

three year contract, herself, Robert and **James Shepherd** clerk and commercial traveller. These partners would be involved with profits of which five-sevenths would go to Mrs Nairn, and one-seventh to each of the other two. Robert remained a traveller with the firm and lived with his mother at the Priory until he died in 1886 at the age of 50, having just retired. He was never very stong and acted as a salesman for the company. Mrs Nairn died in 1891 by which time only three of her children were still alive, John, Michael and Euphemia. The Priory was built around 1880 for Mrs Nairn, Robert and his sisters.

After a few years James Shepherd, although he had become a director and a partner was getting restless and left in 1864. He set up in business with Michael Beveridge and his expertise and Michael Beveridge's money formed the Kirkcaldy Floorcloth Factory in 1865 not very far from Nairn's Pathhead factory.

A new Nairn's contract was formed for a four year period with Michael Barker now one of the partners. It was Michael Barker's expertise that guided the firm through successful expansion over the next 40 years.

In 1868 St Mary's Canvas factory was opened opposite the Harbour for the manufacture of table baize. and extended in 1880. It is now part of Fife College, the Priory Campus.

MICHAEL BARKER NAIRN 1838-1915

Harbour Factories 1869,1880, now Fife College Priory Campus

Dysart House

Michael Barker had been educated at the Burgh School and he recalled the day in 1843 when the school moved into fine new premises at St Brycedale Avenue. He was studying law in Edinburgh and was about to move to London when his father died when he was but 19.

In 1866 he married **Emily Frances Spencer** from Weybridge. They lived in the High Street and later bought St Marys which had belonged to David Landale. The house stood above St Mary's Well, no trace of which appears to remain. The house had been enlarged from a two to a three storey house. The Priory was built closeby St Marys and was where Mrs Nairn, her daughters and Robert lived. Mrs Nairn died in 1891.

Michael Barker had four daughters, **Catherime, Emily Frances, Edith Blanche, and Euphemia** and two sons one **Michael Barker** Junior, born 1874 and a second son **Robert Spencer Nairn**. In 1868 Micheal Barker became a Burgess of Kirkcaldy. Catherine married William Black who died in 1922 but who was followed in the firm by their son William C.G. Black. St Marys was used for a while by Sea Cadets, but was demolished around 1963. The Priory later became flats for Nairn visitors and is now part of Fife College's extension, with a hostel for students built in the grounds.

In the early days the working week was for 60 hours for six days. Later it was to be cut down first to 58 and later to 54 for five and a half days, but if the proposed strike went ahead no worker dismissed would be taken on by any floorcloth manufacturer in Kirkcaldy and the hours would return to 58. In 1869 the red sandstone Grecian style offices were built at the top of the Path and demolished in 1964.

In 1876 Michael Barker bought Rankeillor for a summer residence.and the new Nether Street factory opened in 1877. In 1896 Michael Barker bought Dysart House for a winter residence.

Michael Barker Nairn was knighted in 1904. He gifted the Cottage Hospital to the town in 1890 and its later extensions in 1899 and 1915 which included the two round wards, named Michael and Emily. He set up a Sabbath School for the children of Pathhead and a Working Men's Institute. He gifted the YMCA at the foot of Kirk Wynd as a memorial to Provost Patrick Don Swan in 1901. He aided the building of the new St Brycedale Church in 1877 and gifted two stained glass windows and the organ. He extended the Burgh School in 1894 where a bust of Micheal Barker Nairn was at the door. of the assembly hall,. Pupils entering the hall had to pass underneath his bust. He contributed to a mission for the Free Church in Coal

Cottage Hospital 1890 demolished 1989

Grammar School with extension. Behind can be seen the National Works of the Hendry, Hendry, Whyte and Strachan works

Wynd. Later he bought the ground in Nether Street including in 1900 the Old Dunnikier Free Church, Old Philp School and Smeaton Field for space for the factory to expand. It is on the Smeaton Field, north of the railway line that most of the modern factory is sited.

He died peacefully in November 1915. on a journey from Rankeillor to the Kirkcaldy factory and is buried in Monimail Cemetery as is his wife and other members of his and the Spencer-Nairn family.

Michael Barker Nairn's son also Michael Barker Nairn gifted on behalf of his daughters in 1926, the Deaf and Dumb Institute, opposite the Adam Smith Theatre, now known as the Volunteer Centre. He also gifted the grounds of his Dysart House, the Three Trees Park to the Town of Kirkcaldy in 1929.

JOHN NAIRN 1853-1928

John Nairn was only four when his father died. He became a partner when Robert retired in 1885. In addition to the two Nairn brothers the Board then consisted of **John Forrester, William Black,** who married **Catherine Nairn, William Cairns, William Kidd and James Herd..** John Nairn married **Gladys Couper** 1865-1922

Forth Park home of John Nairn and gifted by his daughter Mrs Wemyss Honeymoon in 1936 for a Maternity Hospital. (Sadly the listed building is closed as it has became dangerous. It is hoped that it will be restored in time.

Kirkcaldy Museum 1925 gifted to Kirkcaldy by John Nairn as part of the War Memorial to the many men who died including his only son Ian. The Library was added by John Nairn in 1928.

John Nairn's only son **Ian Nairn**, Captain in the 4th Hussars of the Fife and Forfar Yeomanry, was tragically killed before the end of the Great War. He had won the Military Medal and bar. Sadly too their daughter Kathleen Jean died when only 39.

In memory of his son John Nairn gave the Museum to Kirkcaldy in 1925 as part of the War Memorial and in 1928 the Library was added. In 1892 he bought Forth Park after Daniel Hendry died. This house his daughter Mrs Wemyss Honeyman later gave to Kirkcaldy in 1936 as a Maternity Home, as well as donating a number of paintings from the family home to the Art Gallery.

Some Nairn's Milestones

1926 Central Power Station built by Sir Michael Junior

1927 Sir Michael Junior bought Dunniker Foundary for a Paper Mill

1939 New Head Offices opened at Braehead House.

1939-45 Manufactured shell and torpedos

Sir Michael Barker Nairn Junior lived in Dysart House until he bought Elie House. He gave the grounds of Dysart House and the grounds and policies of Ravenscraig Castle to the town of Kirkcaldy in 1929. His only son was Michael George Barker Nairn, later Sir Michael Nairn. Dysart House was sold to the Coates of Paisley fame who gifted it to the Carmellites.

1925 Robert Spencer-Nairn was knighted.

1936 Balgeddie House was built for Alastair Spencer-Nairn shortly after he was married. It has been a hotel since around 1964.

1953 Sir Robert Spencer-Nairn gifted the house to the Church of Scotland as an eventide home. It is now being converted into flats.

Braehead House, Head Office until 1989

The Priory 1997

Nairn's List A industrial building Victoria Road. Hopefully it will soon be converted into something useful.

JAMES SHEPHERD
1830-1906

James Shepherd was born in Elgin 1830 and came as a young man as a clerk to Michael Nairn where he had been given posts of responsibility. He was an energetic and hard working young man and his qualities were recognised. After Michael Nairn died in 1858 he became manager and later a Director, but the firm was basically run by the Nairn family. James Shepherd felt that Mrs Nairn and three sons might prove too much for any prospect of better rewards. As a Director he was getting one-seventh of the profits as was Robert, while Mrs Nairn received five-sevenths.

In 1864 with Michael Beveridge who had returned from London he set up the floor covering firm of Shepherd and Beveridge on Factory Road. The building sadly went on fire in 1867 with the loss of two lives. The factory was rebuilt and extended into the Rosslyn Works beside Sinclairtown Station which had once been Johnson's Linen Works. They were so successful that they later expanded into the Lorne and Elgin works, Overton Road and trading after 1877 as the Kirkcaldy Linoleum Company.

Rosslyn works now demolished and flats built.

Rossend Castle c. 1900

James Shepherd Grave, Burntisland

The firm's travelling salesman was John Barry. Mr Edward Ostlere also worked in the office as Secretary at this time. However Mr Shepherd was very displeased with Mr Barry after reading one of his political speeches in the local press fearing that it would harm the business. Mr Barry just walked out and Mr Ostlere followed shortly afterwards. Both left around 1881.

In 1873 James Shepherd bought **Rossend Castle**. He enjoyed sledging and when there was enough snow would sledge into town. He pioneered the local tramways in Kirkcaldy and was one of the first to have electric lights. He was instrumental in setting up and establishing Dodhead Golf Course in Burntisland. He was a very kind man.

He married **Christine Louse Sanguinede** from Geneva who died in 1899 when she was 60 years old. She is buried in Burnisland Cemetery. James Shepherd was also buried there in 1906 dying when he was 70. He had a son **John Ernest Shepherd** (1863-1934) who lived at Nether Grange, Burntisland but who died in Edinburgh aged 61. John Ernest had married **Lilias Jane Welsh** who died in 1944 and was cremated.

James Shepherd also had two daughters **Una Muriel** born in 1868 and **Charlotte Louse** born in 1872.

Kirkcaldy Station around 1900. Note the nearby works

McIntosh's Victoria Cabinet Works, Victoria Road 1880-1970

New Mitcheson Factory, now ESA McIntosh 1970-

ALEXANDER HENRY M'INTOSH
1835-1919

In earlier times the name was spelt M'Intosh and indeed for most of his life that was how **Alexander Henry M'Intosh** spelt his name.

He was born on April 2 1835, and died aged 84 in Kirkcaldy on September 25 1919. During his lifetime he proved himself an able man who rose from very humble origins to be a JP, member of the Kirkcaldy Town Council for a short time, member and chairman of the School Board, leading elder in the Baptist Church and a highly successful furniture manufacturer.

Alexander's great grandfather **Charles** had been a driver on the stagecoach between Edinburgh, Perth and Inverness, and the family from the Highlands had been involved in the massacre at Culloden His grandfather **Thomas** had been an Exciseman in Edinburgh, and married **Janet Hyslop** in 1789 in Newton, Edinburgh.

Alexander's father was **William M'Intosh**, an upholsterer who after being apprenticed in Dalkeith, eventually had a business in the Abbey area of Dunfermline. William's first wife and the mother of Alexander Henry was **Margaret Henry**. They were married at St

52

McIntosh Grave, Bennochy

Award winning McIntosh sideboard of 1878

Cuthbert's Church Edinburgh in 1828 and the oldest of their children **Thomas** was born during the same year. There were three children of the marriage and **Alexander Henry** was the youngest. There was an older brother Thomas, unmarried who died of a fever in early adulthood in 1853 aged 24, who was at that time living and working in the Linktown of Abbotshall.

Little is known about Alexander's mother but she must have died when he was only a few months old as Alexander's father was married again in Dunfermline on January 1 1836. There were several children of that marriage, but nothing is known about them, Alexander's step-brothers and sisters.

Alexander came to Linktown after his brother Thomas died. Thomas worked in the Linktown for Samuel Barnet. Alexander took his place and worked for Samuel Barnet, an Upholster and Cabinet Maker, for many years.

In the Linktown he met **Jane Wishart,** a dressmaker whom he married in 1854 in Abbotshall Parish Church., when he was 19 and she was 26 years old. Their first child **William** was born in 1855. Jane's father was **George Wishart** and her mother **Isabella Glass.**

Alexander and Jane lived in a little house in the Links until 1879, after all their children had been born. They then moved to 18 Russel Place to be near their new factory. Alexander and Jane had a total of seven children., six surviving. William was followed by **Isabella** in **1857, Alexander 1860, Thomas 1861, Margaret 1868** and **George** in 1870.

Alexander Henry M'Intosh worked with the Barnets for 15 years before he struck out and opened up his own business. Alexander was then 34 years old in 1869. His furniture business was at the foot of Whytescauseway and later he had extensions both in Rose Street and at Volunteers' Green. From the large advertisement placed in the Fifeshire Advertiser by A.H.M'Intosh in February 1871 it can be seen that upholstery was sold as well as furniture, carpets, beds, mirrors etc.

Alexander Henry was a good craftsman and knew what good craftsmen were about and valued their work highly. When he started his own business he employed good craftsmen, used good materials and produced a much valued piece of work which might have been expensive but at that time it was not intended for the humbler customer. He knew what his customers wanted. His reputation grew, orders flowed in and the business expanded. He obviously had a good business brain, was open to modern methods of production and had excellent relations with his workforce and customers.

A.H.M'Intosh grew and prospered. One of the reasons being that the railways were opening up the country. Kirkcaldy's Station and line through Fife (Perth Dundee Edinburgh) opened in 1847 and there followed a boom in the hotel trade. The middle class was expanding and people were now able to travel to places in comfort instead of in draughty, slow and unreliable stagecoaches. Hotels opened up in once remote places and accommodation was required for overnight travellers and visitors and so a rash of station hotels, hydros and other hotels grew up. Trade was flourishing in the furnishing of the new hotels. A.H.M'Intosh was deeply involved and soon it was obvious that more space and more room was required so that more modern equipment could be brought in and used and that the three parts of the business could be housed under one roof.

After 10 years when he was 44 A.H. M'Intosh bought a large piece of ground with a railway siding running off at Victoria Road. Many said that this was too far out of town and no one would travel that distance to visit his warehouse to buy his furniture. But they were wrong as this part of the town soon grew and prospered.

Many skilled workmen like Alexander Henry were setting up their own businesses and becoming very quickly rich. Their knowledge of what work was about, with the skills they possessed made them much more successful business men than the spoiled rich upper classes who employed a manager while they played. Managers were very successful at feathering their own nests.

Amongst such self-made men around Kirkcaldy were men like Aytoun of milling fame, Newton Mills, Nicol Street; Andrew Carnegie who made his fortune in America with steel; John Key engineering and ship building in Kirkcaldy and Kinghorn and Alexander Henry M'Intosh. Perhaps the suddenness of their rise to financial success made these men less able to adapt to times when there was a slump in trade and a change in the markets and they often overreached themselves. Not so A.H. M'Intosh, not so Ninian Lockhart but it was so of John Key.

The family moved to 18 Russell Place to be close to the works. The house faced the sea and had a back garden facing onto Victoria Road. It was not until later that the back gardens were sold off and onto the backs of the Russell Place houses were built the smart terraced houses in Victoria Road. At the time of the move William the oldest son was 24 years old and already involved with his father's business. Isabella was 22 and the youngest George was nine years old.

The new factory was built on a greenfield site on the lands of Balsusney and opened in 1880. After the factory was built land was set aside for the house that A.H.M'Intosh intended to build for his family, Victoria House now Victoria Hotel. The family moved in in 1892. The Hotel still retains some of the lovely woodwork especially the staircase bannisters and panelling in the dining room.

In one year a purpose built typical late 19th Century factory was built, which opened in September 1880 was mainly three storeys high with the show rooms, warehouse and factory all in one place.

Timber was brought in here by rail, whole trees mainly from West Africa, walnut, mahogany and obeche and allowed to season slowly. The logs were turned daily. Later a machine to extract some of the moisture was used which speeded up the seasoning process without any loss of quality of the timber or its product. The use of whole trees continued at the new Mitchelston factory and was phased out when the firm went into receivership in 1982. Veneers and chip boards were introduced being cheaper and still giving a professional effect, so timber was used less often This reduced the time the cash was tied up in the slow process of seasoning the timber. Today ready seasoned timber is brought in. as required.

Despite all adverse predictions the M'Intosh factory thrived and boomed from the very beginning. In 1885 A.H. M'Intosh made William his oldest son a Director also Isabella his daughter. Isabella married George Fergusson in 1886 and George Fergusson now acted through her. They lived at that time at 30 Victoria Road and around 1901 the house at the corner of Alexandra Street, Alexandra House. was built for them and their son Patrick George. This house, is now known as Victoria House, while opposite the original Victoria House is the Victoria Hotel.

Soon the factory was not big enough and an extension was made in 1889 as the now defunct works of the Whytebank Engineering Company of John Key were acquired. M'Intosh now owned all the land between the railway and Victoria Road.Whytebank Engineering works had been set up by John Key in 1850 and he was engaged in the large works, making engine parts for ships. The railway siding was there and he was able to transport his materials in and out, especially to his Kinghorn Ship Building yard.

The McIntosh factory was involved making aeroplane parts during both World Wars I and II. After the 1939-45 war there was a big demand for domestic furniture. The need for a modern factory all on one floor, became apparent and after the disastrous hurricane of 1968 a move was made in 1970 to the Mitchelston greenfield site.

The firm of A.H. McIntosh still carries on as E.S.A McIntosh but no longer produces home furniture, having now expanded into the fitted furniture for school science rooms, hospitals and doctors surgeries. Today there are no members of that great family still employed in the firm, the last McIntosh Managing Director being the great grandson of Alexander Henry M'Intosh, George Fergusson who died President of the firm in 1976 having been a very successful Chairman and Managing Director for 14 years, from 1958-1972 (Grandson of M'Intosh's oldest daughter and the first George Fergusson). Grandson William, son of George the youngest M'Intosh son, retired in 1957 but remained on the Board of Directors until 1980 and died in 1996. For a few short months his son Neil was involved with the firm.

Victoria Hotel

MICHAEL BEVERIDGE
1836-90

Michael Beveridge was born in 1836 and died of pneumonia at the age of 54 in 1890. His parents were Alexander Beveridge and Grace Black. He had two older sisters, one of whom was still alive when he died.

Michael Beveridge went from Kirkcaldy to London as a young man, to learn about the business world and worked in insurance and returned to Kirkcaldy in 1864 before he was 30.

Michael Beveridge became a partner with James Shepherd, who had worked for many years with Michael Nairn and knew all about the manufacture of floorcloth. After Michael Nairn died James Shepherd remained with the firm for a while after being made a Director, but felt that with a widow and three sons he would have too much competition to make a fortune. Michael Beveridge had the management skills and the money so that the partnership made a successful investment setting up the Shepherd and Beveridge Floorcloth Company manufacturing floorcloth. The factory was sited in Factory Road.

In 1867 the factory went on fire and two of the workers were killed. Fire was a great hazard of all the new factories especially furniture and floorcloth. However the factory was rebuilt and extended and in 1877 was renamed the Kirkcaldy Linoleum Company. By this time.

Beechwood 1995

Grave of Michael Beveridge and his two wives, Bennochy.

Walton's patent on the name Linoleum having by now expired through default as he omitted to renew the patent hence the change of name from floorcloth to linoleum. The new works were in the Rosslyn Works in Sinclairtown, which had been Johnson's Linen Works but the market for linen was declining.

In 1876 when the small Burghs combined with Kirkcaldy:- Sinclairtown, Gallatown, Linktown and Pathhead he became a Town Councillor and two years later a baillie. Following the retirement of Provost Patrick Don Swan he became Provost in 1887. Sadly Provost Michael Beveridge died in 1890 from pneumonia

The Kirkcaldy Linoleum Company continued under James Shepherd until 1899 when the business merged with Barry and Ostlere, and became Barry, Ostlere and Shepherd.Co. Ltd.

Michael Beveridge purchased the land for Beechwood in 1870 and we have evidence that he was living in the house by 1873. Michael Beveridge had no children. His first wife was **Maud Greig Kay**. who died in May 1883 and shortly afterwards Michael Beveridge married **Elizabeth Hunter Stocks** daughter of the linen manufacturer in the Links who was many years younger than him. She outlived her husband by 48 years dying in 1938.

Michael Beveridge and his two wives are buried with a simple stone along the west side of the dividing wall in the Bennochy Cemetery. It is thought that he married Maud Kay between 1866-70 and she died in 1883, in 1886 he married Elizabeth Hunter Stocks.

He was a member of St Brycedale Church and also had a seat in the General Assembly of the Church of Scotland.

Politically Michael Beveridge was a Gladstonian Liberal and a member of the local Radical Association. He was also a member of the School Board and took special pains to make sure that the schools were well maintained.

When he died he was also the Chairman of a Committee which was set up to honour Kirkcaldy's greatest son, Adam Smith, indeed one of the World's leading economists studied today by many people the world over, especially the Japanese.

Michael Beveridge died in 1890 nine years before Adam Smith Halls were opened in 1899 by Andrew Carnegie of Skibo Castle (and Dunfermline) incorporating the Beveridge Library which remained there until the Kirkcaldy Library was opened in 1928 donated by John Nairn of Forth Park in memory of the deaths of 1012 men during World War I and of his only son Ian.. The Beveridge books moved to the new premises in 1928 and the rooms in the Adam

Adam Smith Halls, now Adam Smith Theatre

Original Bandstand, which disappeared in 1957.

Smith Theatre became the Beveridge Hall, then the Beveridge Suite.

Before he died Michael Beveridge had already made available in his will a gift of £50,000 to be used to create a Park and a Library for the people of Kirkcaldy.

The Beveridge Park was formed from land purchased from Raith Estate, the Newton Park at the top of the Newton (Nicol Street) and the nearby Robbie's Park, and was opened on 24 September 1892. There are two similar plaques on each of the Park gates:-

"This Park was provided out of money bequeathed for the purpose to the Provost, Magistrates and Town Council of Kirkcaldy by Michael Beveridge of Beechwood who died Provost of Kirkcaldy 4th March 1890."

"This Park was opened by Mrs Beveridge the widow of the donor along with the Provost, Magistrates and Town Council of the Burgh of Kirkcaldy on the 24th September 1892"

In 1992 a similar Centenary celebration equalling or even greater than the original one, took place in the Park with the 'Dancing Waters' with "tea and biscuits" in the Town House afterwards. Originally there had been 10,000 in the Park followed by "tea and buns" in the Town House.

The fountain' was erected in 1931 by Mrs E.H. Beveridge "In Memory of her husband, Provost Michael Beveridge the Donor of the Park". Sadly the ornamental gates were scrapped as part of the war effort (probably also the cannon) and the beautiful bandstand disappeared around the late 1950's.

In 1992, the Provost and Kirkcaldy Civic Society planted trees in the Park, near the Main Gate, on September 24 1992 and there is a plaque below the copper beech planted for the Civic Society by Mr William Yule, first Chairman of the Society. The tree is growing well (Main Gates on right of boundary, a few yards from the gate)

After Mrs Beveridge died in 1938 Beechwood was used to billet Polish Soldiers during the war years.

After World War II, the Royal British Legion bought the house and created extra halls and two bowling greens. Lack of old soldiers and changes in people's social habits resulted in the building being too costly to maintain. The turf of the bowling green was sold and flats built in the grounds, Legion Court with the big house converted into two luxury flats, Beechwood Court. Kirkcaldy Civic Society has replaced the plaque on the door of Beechwood having originally sited it in 1992.

Fountain presented by Mrs Beveridge in 1931 in memory of her husband. It is topped by a beaver, part of the Beveridge family coat of arms.

Lodge and Main Gate to Beveridge Park

JOHN BARRY
1846-1921

John Barry was born in Ireland at Bannow Co. Wexford in 1846 and lived there until his father, who was a lighthouse keeper, was moved to Northumberland and he continued his schooling in Newcastle. It is said that he used to salt herrings after school for 4d an hour (todays money about 2p)

It was said that on one occasion he called on a banker who would not normally have agreed to see him, but the name rang a bell and he asked if John Barry was the wild young man he had known at Newcastle. The reply came, "yes I was that imp and you were the scholar".

He was first employed in the drapery business, Dunn's of Newcastle later moving to carpets in Bainbridge where he first met Mr Shepherd and was "spotted". Later it was James Shepherd who invited him to Scotland to work as a travelling salesman for the Shepherd and Beveridge Floorcloth Company. When in Newcastle he met Mr William Sutton, older than himself but they became firm friends and it was with Mr Sutton's help that the Barry and Ostlere company was established.

John Barry later left Shepherd and Beveridge and set up with Edward Ostlere in the old Patent Floorcloth Company works near the station which had been abandoned since a fire. Later they absorbed the space of Tait, Chorley and Company, the North Floorcloth Factory and Hendry, Whyte and Strachan (Walton,

Bennochy Park 1997

Forth House

Caledonia and Abbotshall works). Finally the Kirkcaldy Linoleum Company, formerly Shepherd and Beveridge, merged in 1899 to form the linoleum firm of Barry, Ostlere and Shepherd, exporting at one time all over the world. Sadly the factory closed in 1964. The expansion into fitted carpets was partly responsible, there not being room in Kirkcaldy for more than one large linoleum manufacturing firm.

John Barry was not technical but was commercially minded and he had a flamboyant life style. He fell out with Shepherd when employed at Shepherd and Beveridge, after a particularly bold press report on the Irish question, Shepherd claiming that this publicity would be the ruin of the firm and so they parted. Later however Shepherd's Company merged with that of Barry and Ostlere and became the well known Barry, Ostlere and Shepherd. The massive works along Forth Avenue were eventually demolished and the ground attractively landscaped in the late 1970's. None of the firm's buildings were purpose-built like Nairn or McIntosh.. They bought up the old buildings and at one time owned at least a dozen spread around Kirkcaldy. Forth House, once Barry, Ostlere and Shepherd's head office, having originally been Jeffreys' Linen Mill, is now Fife Council, Central Area Planning Office.

John Barry was a great reader, a supporter of free trade, a political activist, a supporter of the Roman Catholic faith and a JP. He was generous to all charities. He was a Member of Parliament for Wexford representing the Irish Republican Party in 1890. John Barry lived in Bennochy Park, now an Abbeyfield House. He was married and had a son. He died in 1921 in London at the age of 75.

It is thought that before he was married he lived at Wester Torbain house and was looked after by a manservant.

Chapel House, now Dean Park Hotel, 1997

Ostlere Graves Kinghorn and Hayfield

EDWARD OSTLERE
1848-1902

Edward Ostlere was born in Howden Yorkshire in 1848 and was for many years Managing Director of Barry Ostlere and Company.

His business experience began with working for a carpet firm in London and in 1877 he joined the Esher Linoleum Company as manager. At this time Shepherd and Beveridge were acquiring the Johnson's old Sinclairtown Linen Factory. Both Barry and Ostlere were engaged at the firm with Shepherd and Beveridge, where Mr John Barry was salesman and Mr Edward Ostlere Secretary.

However in 1881 both Barry and Ostlere left to set up their own company, with help of a financial investment from Mr Sutton a longtime friend of Mr Barry

In 1887 the Barry and Ostlere Company acquired Caledonian Works from Tait Cairns and Co. Ltd, took over North British Works and later the National Works.

Mr Edward Ostlere had two brothers later in the business, Mr Fred and Mr Arthur. Edward's great hobby was horses and breeding horses. He was a great family man, kind and generous. At one time he was a tenant of Pitteadie Farm. and it was there that his wife died He had married Mary Sophia Smith who died in 1880 aged 33. He was always punctual, thoughtful, kind and generous. His two sons were also in the business, Eric and Harold.

Edward Ostlere lived in Chapel House and was well known in farming circles and bred horses. He died in 1902 after a "lingering illness" aged only 54. He is buried in Kinghorn cemetery with his wife who died when she was only 32, an infant son who died at 6 weeks and his son Eric who died in 1958 aged 82

Other members of the family are buried in Hayfield. Mr Harold Ostlere, his son, who lived at Marchmont (1880-1938) is buried in Hayfield and his son killed on active service during World War II is remembered on the stone, Flight Lieutenant Edward Ostlere aged 28, also Christine who died in Ocotber 1961, the widow of Ft.Lieut. Edward Ostlere.(?)

BIBLIOGRAPHY

Barry, Ostlere, and Shepherd Magazine
"Century of Progress 1838-1938" Lockhart
"Fife Shopkeepers and Traders 1820-70" Campbell 1989
"Hutchisons of Kirkcaldy" 1984
"Industries, Kirkcaldy and District 1870" Bryson 1872
"Linen and Flax in Kirkcaldy" Livingstone 1951
"Lockhart, 150 years of Progress and Development" 1949
"McIntosh Story" Ann Watters 1995
"Monumental Stones in Fife" Mitchell and Mitchell 1970
"Nairns of Kirkcaldy 1847-1956" Augustus Muir 1956
"Past at Work Around the Lomonds" George Bennett
"Whytes of Bennochy" Vol.XII.2 Scottish Genealogy August 1995

Census Returns

Old Parish Records

Local Graveyard Records

Old Newspapers

Old Maps